BIG
IDEAS
FOR SMALL
SPACES

ROCKPORT

BIG
IDEAS
FOR SMALL
SPACES

CHRISTINE BRUN ABDELNOUR

GLOUCESTER MASSACHUSETTS

ROCKPORT PUBLISHERS

First published in the United States of America by
Rockport Publishers, Inc.
33 Commercial Street
Gloucester, Massachusetts 01930-5089
Telephone: (978) 282-9590
Facsimile: (978) 283-2742

ISBN 1-56496-607-0

10 9 8 7 6 5 4 3 2 1

Design: Stoltze Design, Boston.
Cover image: Photo by Henry Bourne, design by Powell-Tuck Associates.
Back cover images as follows: Top right: photo by Eric A. Roth; bottom left: photo by Jeff McNamara, design by Austin Patterson Disston; bottom right: photo by Sam Gray Photography, design by Bierly-Drake.

Printed in China.

contents

planning

FOR SMALL SPACES

Small living spaces present big challenges. The trick is to address maintenance and function without sacrificing aesthetics. The architect Mies van der Rohe declared that "less is more." And indeed he was known for reducing an object to its essentials and then polishing the design with attention to details—the kind of details that make a difference when space is at a premium. But you don't have to be a famous architect to make the most of a small space.

Start by listing your specific needs; include the sizes of things you'll need to store or accommodate. The easiest method is to grab a rigid tape measure and write down each object's height, width, and depth. If something must open to function, allow for the space it needs, plus the area required for your hand to move. Take notes on how much space things occupy, even if they're currently spread out over several rooms. If you have books all over, for instance, measure their total linear feet. Remember that the secret weapon of small space is vertical space. If you can make use of every inch—floor to ceiling, wall to wall, over doors, and under windows—the walls expand. Make your list very accurate and detailed, and include photos of pieces that you want to use.

Look for built-in possibilities under windows, as seen here, and over doors. While you might not have room for large bookshelves, you can sneak smaller sections into your home to produce adequate storage space.

PHOTOGRAPHY
ERIC A. ROTH

Change traditional swinging doors to sliding pocket doors, and gain 8 to 10 valuable square feet (.75 to .9 square meters) around the door for more flexible furniture placement.

Next, measure the available floor space. Professional designers always create scale floor plans, usually at 1/4-inch (.5 cm) scale. If you can, begin your actual planning on paper, either manually or with the aid of a computer program. You may need to consult with a professional designer to produce a functional furniture plan. It might cost several hundred dollars, but it can save thousands. Many clients have called me only after squandering their furnishings budget on an expensive blunder. Once you see how much floor area is available, you can establish sizes for individual pieces. Check the pieces you want to keep against the layout to see if they work well—it's certainly easier than physically moving the furniture around the house. Go shopping with your furniture layout, several copies of the blank floor plans, and a scale ruler.

Now, you can begin to utilize the vertical space that is left over. Look into the ingenious space-saving products on the home-improvement market: sliding pocket doors, retractable hardware, spiral staircase kits, refrigerated drawers, under-counter washers and dryers, collapsible outdoor furniture, compact fireplaces, and pullout kitchen tables. Investigate custom-designed, built-in features, which can have a huge impact in a tiny room. Inches make a difference, and in a compact space, built-in features can elevate the mundane to the extraordinary. Frank Lloyd Wright believed that a house should be one consistent flow of space; he used integrated storage, seating, and tables in his work, blending architecture and furniture. This continuity is easy for the eye to accept, and it gives the viewer a sense of harmony. Small spaces beg to be unified; they blossom when they're designed to be tight, precise, and well integrated.

Products such as this updated trundle bed offer function and space-saving solutions without sacrificing style. The Italian design allows for two twin beds in the floor space of one. With slip-covers and bolsters, the bed becomes a simple, sleek contemporary sofa.

PHOTOGRAPHY
DORMIRE

Finally, rid yourself of old notions about what a room should be like. Furniture can roll around or change heights and shapes to serve several needs. The coffee table can rise to dining height. You can have bookcases in your dining room or a dining room out on the deck. Odd shapes below stairs and tiny corners beside windows can become a home for books or art objects, once you install appropriate-size shelves. Even your bedroom can serve extra functions; there are beds that lift up to reveal a storage compartment or that feature drawers below the mattress. Armoires open up to become computer workstations and little home offices.

"A small house well-filled is better than an empty palace," a wise person once said. While you may have limited opportunities to declare your individual style in a small home, make every brushstroke count. The first step is identifying chances to express yourself. Five or six inches of wall between two double-hung windows could host a collection of antique cookie molds, or a display of small plates might fit over a doorway. If there's only room for a love seat and a table in your apartment, make them special. Deliberate over the color and texture of fabric; choose wood that you love; seek out appealing shapes. You can invent a functional and aesthetically enticing home within 450 square feet (42 square meters) if you forget about old patterns. Adopt ideas from industry or the office. Give yourself permission to invest in just the right pieces to make the puzzle fit. Good planning, coupled with a little ingenuity, can produce sparkling answers to the challenge of small spaces.

Spiral-staircase kits fit into a square or round well opening only 2 inches (5 cm) larger than the diameter of the staircase. You need only 44 inches (112 cm) to connect a loft space to the rest of your living area. In that space, you can carve out guest quarters or a little office/study area.

Adopt simple solutions that fit the architecture. Here, narrow shelves are crafted to snuggle into a tight corner in a tiny bungalow kitchen.

PHOTOGRAPHY
BRADY ARCHITECTURAL PHOTOGRAPHY
DESIGN
LAURA BIRNS, ASID

To make an extra "room," turn a porch into a comfortable seating area.

PHOTOGRAPHY
CHRIS SHIPLEY
DESIGN
JOHN KELLY

Keep an eye out for opportunities to express your individual sense of style. Here, a narrow vertical scrap of wall becomes a marvelous, concise display space for clock faces.

PHOTOGRAPHY
SAM GRAY PHOTOGRAPHY
DESIGN
BIERLY-DRAKE

Free yourself from preconceived ideas and let a room become whatever you need it to be at the moment. This dining room features comfortable chairs that can be turned for use in the living room and built-in shelves rather than a buffet or china cabinet.

PHOTOGRAPHY
ERIC A. ROTH
DESIGN
PETER WHEELER

Plan out furniture arrangements, and select pieces that fit the space in size as well as style.

PHOTOGRAPHY
STEVE VIERRA PHOTOGRAPHY
DESIGN
DIANE HUGHES

Steal living space from adjacent outdoor decks or balconies. A small bedroom or living room can expand onto these areas to give a sense of increased space.

PHOTOGRAPHY
COLL PHOTOGRAPHY
DESIGN
DOREE FRIEDMAN

color IN SMALL SPACES

Color is compelling; don't be afraid to design with it in a small interior. While it is generally true that dark hues and values makes spaces seem closer and light values make space recede, avoiding color is not a requirement for well-dressed small spaces. All-white or neutral rooms—popularized by the famed Elsie de Wolfe in America and Syrie Maugham in England, and later by the Modernist Movement in architecture—are not the only option.

Understanding its qualities and properties will inspire you to use color with confidence. Large blocks of color can set the mood for a room, and no other design element is quite as influential (or economical). Success with color depends on a good recipe: An intense color can be used on the wall if the floor is the same color or one that blends the walls and floor together. Sometimes swathing the entire room in color results in a comforting effect that complements the tiny stature of a space.

Choosing accent colors for specific room elements—walls, floors, upholstery fabrics, or artwork—is another way to weave color into compact environments. Minimal use of very intense color will magnify its appeal in an otherwise neutral interior. While there is no "right" or "wrong" color to select, the basic properties (cool colors soothe and retreat, warm colors advance and excite) will help you choose well.

Designing a comfortable room using a single color—for instance, all browns or a palette of gold—offers its own challenges and rewards. The danger, as in the infamous all-white room, is that the result will be bland and lack punctuation; the space may fall flat. Vary hues, experimenting with quantity, patterns and solids, and light and dark colors. And remember: In a small space, a color's impact is magnified.

PHOTOGRAPHY | **GREY CRAWFORD** | DESIGN | **JEFFREY ALAN MARKS**

Color can be used to sculpt and identify blocks of space in a small area. Juxtaposing two complements, such as these deep-red walls with apple green through the room beyond, establishes a sense of distance and makes the space look inviting.

Use crisp, white trim against walls bathed in green, a soothing color, to deliver an atmosphere of freshness in a cramped space. Keep expanses of a single color from looking opaque by rag rolling, combing, or adding other subtle texture to the wall; this lets paler tones show through and helps reflect light. A tiny room firmly assumes a comfortable personality appropriate to its purpose.

PHOTOGRAPHY
GREY CRAWFORD
DESIGN
JEFFREY ALAN MARKS

(right) Humanize small floor areas with high ceilings by bringing the focus down with bold colors at the living level.

PHOTOGRAPHY
CAROL PEERCE
DESIGN
DAWN P. SULLIVAN, ALLIED MEMBER ASID

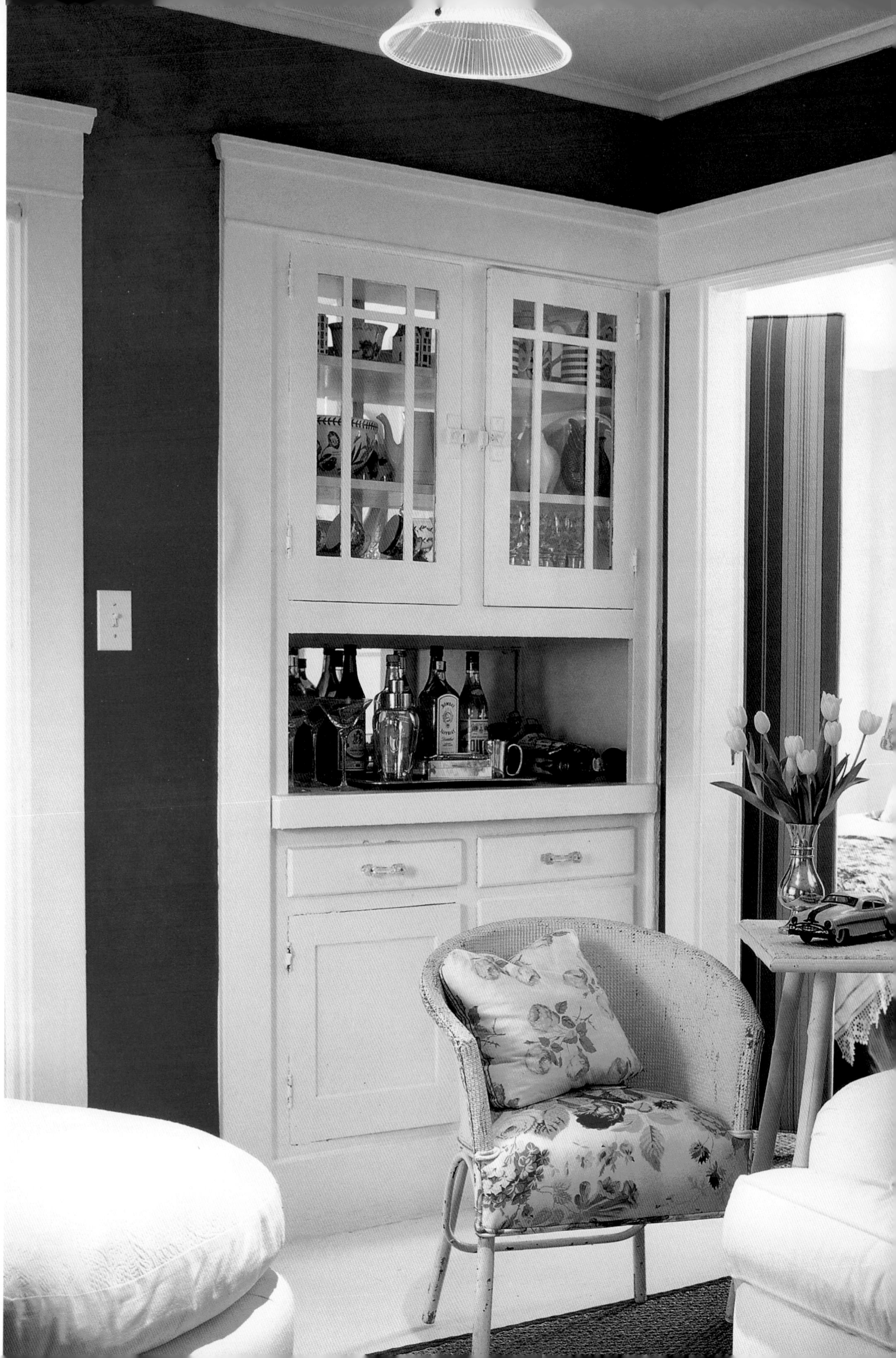

PHOTOGRAPHY | **GREY CRAWFORD** | DESIGN | **JEFFREY ALAN MARKS**

The all-white color scheme has become a small-space cliché. Instead, try pure white woodwork to emphasize bold use of color. Blended and reiterated in the carpet and fabric patterns of pillows and upholstery fabrics, white adds light and an easy flow to a room. Here, the exceptional décor is also economical, relying most on the use of paint to create ambiance.

Use a large canvas painted with a bold color to transform a sterile-feeling apartment. It's portable, economical, and takes up very little room while adding ambiance to your home.

PHOTOGRAPHY
B & B ITALIA

Let a simple painted wall act
as a headboard for a bed,
which in this case is flanked by
crisp, white recessed book
niches and completed with
sconce reading lights.

PHOTOGRAPHY
ERIC A. ROTH
DESIGN
GARY WOLF ARCHITECTS, INC.

A four-color palette is visible when you walk in the door of this 1,097-square-foot (102-square-meter) bungalow. Be daring and brave with your color for an economical design element. Paint takes up no space and delivers a big impact.

PHOTOGRAPHY
BRADY ARCHITECTURAL PHOTOGRAPHY
DESIGN
LAURA BIRNS, ASID

Fabric panels can instantly add color and are temporary, making them ideal for use in rental units. Try a quilt or a vintage drapery panel. You can hang kimonos, batiks, weavings, and old lace from a wide variety of devices, all of which add interest but not clutter.

PHOTOGRAPHY
ERIC A. ROTH
DESIGN
PETER WHEELER

Experiment with unusual colors and wall treatments. Here, deep-red upholstered walls render a diminutive powder bath jewel-like.

PHOTOGRAPHY
MARY E. NICHOLS
DESIGN
CHARLOTTE JENSEN, ASID

Making a room monochromatic,
as this elegant example illustrates,
expands the sense of space.

PHOTOGRAPHY
STEVE VIERRA PHOTOGRAPHY
DESIGN
MANUEL DeSANTIRCH

When you have a limited number of furniture pieces and wall space, make each object count toward your color scheme. Repeat color in your accessories, as shown here.

PHOTOGRAPHY
GREY CRAWFORD
DESIGN
JEFFREY ALAN MARKS

Intensity plays a big role in using color correctly. Here, very strong, saturated goldenrod wraps a breakfast room in sunshine. Brave use of this color disguises boxy architecture and small windows; the splash of bright color makes a simple, upbeat statement. Nuances are another matter in color language, especially with yellow. Choose carefully, and paint a test swatch to make sure that, on the wall, your "cheerful" yellow doesn't become "agitating."

PHOTOGRAPHY
GREY CRAWFORD
DESIGN
JEFFREY ALAN MARKS

Even in a small home office, you can bring life to the walls by using background-colored wall covering. A crackle craft paper was used in this room, but feel free to experiment with different textures of vinyl, natural weaves, and paper-backed fabrics.

PHOTOGRAPHY
ED GOHLICH
DESIGN
MARYCLARE BRANDT, ASID

Architectural elements that define this small kitchen and dining area are painted in an accent hue to complement artwork. The judicious use of color relieves the all-white walls without closing in the space.

PHOTOGRAPHY
BRADY ARCHITECTURAL PHOTOGRAPHY
DESIGN
MICHAEL BORELLI

Think of window treatments as a way to add color to a small room. You can introduce a stark contrast to the walls, as seen here, or blend the walls with a fabric in the same color family. Try patterns with multiple colors for even more impact.

PHOTOGRAPHY
ERIC A. ROTH
DESIGN
C + J KATZ STUDIO

Use color in a limited quantity in a black-and-white environment and still achieve a big accent effect. The result is crisp, clean, and fresh.

PHOTOGRAPHY
BRADY ARCHITECTURAL PHOTOGRAPHY
DESIGN
LAURA BIRNS, ASID

Sometimes all you need is a few isolated spots of bright color to give a small room spark. This room looks colorful, but it's not overwhelming.

PHOTOGRAPHY
KIM BRUN STUDIOS
DESIGN
MARSHA SEWELL, ASID

Intense color can work even in a small area. Try bathing your walls with strong color, as seen here. Then, punctuate the room with sharp accents, like this blue glass bowl in the powder bath and the artwork hung on the wall.

PHOTOGRAPHY
GLEN CORMIER
DESIGN
CHARLOTTE JENSEN, ASID

One advantage to small rooms is
that they can have a cozy feel.
Here, intense blue wraps this
room in comfort.

PHOTOGRAPHY
STEVE VIERRA PHOTOGRAPHY

Try to select patterns that are
appropriate for small areas. You
can mix patterns, as demon-
strated here, as long as the
rhythm is correct.

PHOTOGRAPHY
STEVE VIERRA PHOTOGRAPHY
DESIGN
ANTHONY CATALFANO

PHOTOGRAPHY | **BRADY ARCHITECTURAL PHOTOGRAPHY** | DESIGN | **BAST/WRIGHT INTERIORS**

Colored light bathes an entry hall, drawing attention away from its narrowness and beckoning toward the main living area. Well-lit artwork breaks the sterility of the space.

PHOTOGRAPHY | ERIC A. ROTH | DESIGN | ROBERT MIKLOS

The neutral color scheme seen here—white, black, and gray—gives emphasis to the architectural details and creates an orderly background, all of which adds to the sense of space. The fairly dark shade of gray keeps the room from looking dull, resulting in a strong but subtle effect.

Even a 30-inch high (76 cm) section of wall can make an impact when objects are positioned below it, as this small buffet top demonstrates.

PHOTOGRAPHY
GREY CRAWFORD
DESIGN
JEFFREY ALAN MARKS

Wall coverings deliver color to the room and become an integral part of the color scheme without infringing on available space.

PHOTOGRAPHY
SAM GRAY PHOTOGRAPHY
DESIGN
BIERLY-DRAKE

PHOTOGRAPHY | BRADY ARCHITECTURAL PHOTOGRAPHY | DESIGN | DIANE HARSCH

Illuminated glass, however small in area, expands space and suggests rooms beyond what is visible. Here, built-in glass shelves float a delicate display area and extend a small, U-shaped kitchen. The creative blend of ribbed glass and dark backsplash in a simple design adds to the illusion of depth.

Mirror is an unbeatable interior finish material that creates an illusion of space. Used with skill, mirrors can go almost unnoticed—while the atmosphere they create is appreciated. Exercise care to avoid reflecting ugly joints, utilitarian shelf brackets or unexpected revelations from neighboring areas.

Mirror can have backing of plain silver, bronze, antique finish, or smoke. Applications include the front of cabinetry; between counter surfaces and upper cabinets; wall to wall in bathrooms; or on a closet door. The doors in a narrow passage and the interior surfaces of bookcases can be sheathed in mirror to increase the illusion of space. Masking structural columns, chases for heating and plumbing, or other undesirable architectural features with mirror will not remove them from a room but will certainly make them less noticeable.

The same principle is true of artificial lighting; in confined spaces, the magic of artificial light creates the illusion of dimension and makes the actual floor area appear larger. Layering light in a room delivers depth to the space. Combining a floor uplight (hidden behind a plant), an overhead ceiling fixture, and a halogen reading lamp will paint the room with ambient light, accent and mood light, and task-oriented light. Mirrors and light are a melody and rhythm that can play in any room, regardless of size, and expand the dimension of a place without moving any walls.

expanding space
WITH MIRRORS AND LIGHT

Mirrors can serve as artwork while at the same time opening up a room. Choose a heavy, carved frame for emphasis, and determine the best size for the wall.

PHOTOGRAPHY
ERIC A. ROTH
DESIGN
GREGG CANN

Add light by perforating a wall with windows. This room presents a lovely rhythm of daylight that expands the space, with mirrors used in both traditional and whimsical ways. Try propping up a mirror any place that begs for sparkle.

PHOTOGRAPHY
ERIC A. ROTH
DESIGN
GREG CANN

This room is a sleek example of the use of mirrors and lighting to expand an area. Include incandescent uplights above cabinets for depth, or try low-voltage strip lights in the kick base of cabinets.

expanding space with mirrors and light

PHOTOGRAPHY | **BRADY ARCHITECTURAL PHOTOGRAPHY** | DESIGN | **DIANE HARSCH**

Shoji screens transform light into a luminous glow. You can use this concept of diffuse light in narrow space; work with sand-blasted glass, semi-opaque fabrics, or shoji-like plastic material from Japan.

PHOTOGRAPHY
CHARLOTTE JENSEN, ASID
DESIGN
CHARLOTTE JENSEN, ASID

Lighting adds sparkle to the stunning color and art in this 1,000-square-foot (93-square-meter) condo. The view from inside a tiny galley kitchen is dramatic and gallery-like.

PHOTOGRAPHY/DESIGN
CHARLOTTE JENSEN, ASID

Sculpture and art appear to pop away from the wall when lit properly from above, changing the dynamics of a small space. Try giving your artwork a dark background, and provide low-voltage halogen bulbs for the best and most intense light. Adjustable fixture heads allow for proper positioning of the light beam.

PHOTOGRAPHY/DESIGN
CHARLOTTE JENSEN, ASID

These windows pierce solid walls, allowing the room to "stretch." You can add windows with muntins, single lights, or specialty glass inserts.

PHOTOGRAPHY
SAM GRAY PHOTOGRAPHY
DESIGN
BIERLY-DRAKE

Light the face of a fireplace from above to add dimension. Create a focal wall by using recessed lights—position them two to three feet from the wall you want to accent.

PHOTOGRAPHY
ED GOHLICH
DESIGN
MARYCLARE BRANDT

This room demonstrates another successful union of windows, glass, and artificial lighting to build transparency and expand a confined dining area.

PHOTOGRAPHY
CAROL PEERCE
DESIGN
MARSHA SEWELL, ASID

Limited space means limited surface area for displaying art. These shallow niches offer the light a windowed wall would, with space to arrange valuable collections. Focal lighting can be added for dramatic emphasis, transforming each aperture into sculptural space. Together, these diminutive openings form a strong, luminous whole.

PHOTOGRAPHY
MARY E. NICHOLS
DESIGN
CHARLOTTE JENSEN, ASID

Here, a tiny dressing table hugs a flush mirror installation, and suddenly the bathroom expands. Consider a clean installation from the countertop to the ceiling for maximum effect.

PHOTOGRAPHY
STEVE VIERRA PHOTOGRAPHY
DESIGN
BEV RIVKIND

Install mirror under the cabinets to make a small bar area feel larger.

PHOTOGRAPHY
STEVE VIERRA PHOTOGRAPHY
DESIGN
SUSAN LEFKOWITZ

A mirrored wall offers an unobstructed view to the rest of the living area and patio windows beyond. A custom glass poker table enhances the light, airy feeling.

PHOTOGRAPHY
BRADY ARCHITECTURAL PHOTOGRAPHY
DESIGN
LAURA BIRNS, ASID

Cleverly placed sconce lights can make a simple archway a grand design element. This lighting plan also has the benefit of drawing attention upward, making the space seem dramatically larger.

PHOTOGRAPHY
COLL PHOTOGRAPHY
DESIGN
DOREE FRIEDMAN

The entrance of an apartment or townhouse that has no formal foyer can feel rather abrupt. Try covering a wall in the entry with a mirror. In this case, it serves as a background for a gracious console table.

PHOTOGRAPHY
BRADY ARCHITECTURAL PHOTOGRAPHY
DESIGN
KATHLEEN ZBACNIK, ASID

Creative and geometric,
a stepped mirror application on
a lavatory wall wonderfully reflects
the texture of silk wall covering
and colorful art and seems to
double the size of the room.

PHOTOGRAPHY
BRADY ARCHITECTURAL PHOTOGRAPHY
DESIGN
ANJUM RAZVI, ASID
BRENDA LANZA, ASID

Paired with mirror work, a wrap-around counter offers space for displaying decorative pieces as well as for functional items such as towels.

PHOTOGRAPHY
KIM BRUN PHOTOGRAPHY
DESIGN
CHRISTINE BRUN ABDELNOUR

built-in

FEATURES

When you design a cramped area, inches count; precision and ingenuity are your tools. The riddle of clever space utilization can be answered by using built-in features. First, analyze what the space should accomplish. Do you want to store or hide something? Do you require it to serve a double function? Is it for a private purpose, such as sleeping and grooming, or a more public one, like dining? Second, compile an inventory of the specific items to be accommodated: books, computer equipment, hobby supplies, CD player, television, appliances. Always have the complete dimensions readily available. Third, clear your mind of preconceived notions about room use, and make way for flexible thinking.

A typical 2-foot-by-6-foot (61 by 183 cm) closet in a guest bedroom can be transformed into a dresser or become a closet and kitchenette for a guest, concealed behind attractive bi-fold doors. An illusion of foreshortening occurs when the last 30 inches (76 cm) of a long, narrow room gain sleek shelves for a television and CD player with mirrored closet doors. The space above a sink becomes a floating display for delicate glass pieces with the addition of wall-to-wall glass shelves. Artful management of building materials transforms square walls into angles and shapes that roll out, pull apart, or slide up and down. Beds drop out of upholstered cupboards. Storage drawers hide beneath beds, and file drawers disguise themselves behind colorful panels.

Use materials appropriate to the character and style of your home to blend and conceal double functions. The prescription for success with a built-in unit includes proper scale, uninterrupted lines and connected elements, and careful planning.

PHOTOGRAPHY | **JEFF McNAMARA** | DESIGN | **AUSTIN PATTERSON DISSTON**

A built-in cupboard can have lots of personality. Here, the designer cut slats in the front panels to give them a lighter look and backed them with textured fabrics. You can add color or patterns, too.

Consider a recessed niche for a built-in buffet. Here, it delivers a perfect spot to showcase art in a tiny breakfast nook.

PHOTOGRAPHY
MARY E. NICHOLS
DESIGN
CHARLOTTE JENSEN, ASID

Make your guests feel completely at home with a built-in dresser, hanging storage, and a place for luggage that can be closed off from the rest of a second bedroom. When you don't have guests, you can use the room as a spacious retreat, one uncluttered by a dresser and luggage rack.

PHOTOGRAPHY
BRADY ARCHITECTURAL PHOTOGRAPHY
DESIGN
KATHLEEN M. ZBACNIK, ASID

PHOTOGRAPHY | BRADY ARCHITECTURAL PHOTOGRAPHY | DESIGN | LIINDA MEDINA, ASID, AND MARYLIN MATSON

Recess a flexible file system into the wall, as seen on the left side of this narrow room. Include as many shallow shelves as possible for maximum storage in a home office.

Apartment dwellers can also reap the benefits of custom built-ins. Add color to walls while taking advantage of the ingenuity of European wall systems, and take it with you when you move. Hang open or closed shelves, book-cases, glass shelves, and cabinets.

PHOTOGRAPHY
POLIFORM

A small living room usually means one wall for T.V., CD player, books, and display. You can make an artful arrangement that imitates custom built-ins by utilizing a wall-hung furniture system. Focus the center of the furniture arrangement on the dominant storage unit.

PHOTOGRAPHY
POLIFORM

The bottom of a built-in unit can provide hidden storage for games, photographs, and paperwork. Show off your favorite collection on its upper shelves; the display can change with your moods.

PHOTOGRAPHY
ERIC A. ROTH
DESIGN
KEN KELLEHER

A classic window seat offers
additional seating in a cramped
kitchen or dining room.

PHOTOGRAPHY
ERIC A. ROTH

PHOTOGRAPHY | ERIC A. ROTH | DESIGN | RICHARD EUSTICE

Bring bookshelves right to the edge of windows, and cover every inch of available wall space. Here, a library corner provides an inviting backdrop.

Design book nooks into the
architecture, as done here.
Anticipate your needs while
building, and you can integrate
this kind of feature seamlessly.

PHOTOGRAPHY
BRADY ARCHITECTURAL PHOTOGRAPHY
DESIGN
KATHLEEN M. ZBACNIK, ASID

Two types of built-in solutions
are showcased here: an art
niche pierced through a thick-
ened wall and recessed wood
shelves over flush lower cabinet
doors. Remember to add down-
ward-pointing lights to achieve
dimension and create a useful
display area.

PHOTOGRAPHY
COLL PHOTOGRAPHY
DESIGN
DOREE FRIEDMAN

Paired with Windsor chairs and
an old farm table, this built-in
kitchen seating creates a cozy,
family-oriented space for meals.

PHOTOGRAPHY
STEVE VIERRA PHOTOGRAPHY
DESIGN
SOIKELI + COMPANY

(right) Analyze your shelving use,
and make it as adaptable as possible. You can gain flexibility by
making shelves totally adjustable,
as in this well-designed pantry.

PHOTOGRAPHY
JEFF McNAMARA
DESIGN
AUSTIN PATTERSON DISSTON

Tuck a display shelf over a door. Don't forget about these opportunities to sneak in shelves. With them, you can create delightful visual surprises in your home.

PHOTOGRAPHY
COLL PHOTOGRAPHY
DESIGN
DOREE FRIEDMAN

Put a high display shelf in the tiniest of bedrooms. You can arrange stuffed animals, college memorabilia, or decorative photo boxes on it.

PHOTOGRAPHY
ERIC A. ROTH
DESIGN
DAWN SOUTHWORTH + DANA SALVO

Custom design may offer the best built-in solution to your space crunch. Here, a custom armoire in three parts can be moved around to fit different space requirements.

PHOTOGRAPHY
KIM BRUN STUDIOS
DESIGN
CAROL G. BROWN, ASID

Unify space by blending built-in
features with architectural details.
Here, the doors and moldings
have the same stain as the custom shelving and cabinetry.

PHOTOGRAPHY
STEVE VIERRA PHOTOGRAPHY
DESIGN
ANN LENOX

Built-in features are wonderful for increasing efficiency in a small kitchen. Here, a stove hood doubles as storage and functional condiment ledge.

PHOTOGRAPHY
JEFF McNAMARA
DESIGN
AUSTIN PATTERSON DISSTON

Create a sleeping alcove with practical shelves tucked under a mattress.

PHOTOGRAPHY
STEVE VIERRA PHOTOGRAPHY
DESIGN
MIRIAN GLASGOW

PHOTOGRAPHY | ERIC A. ROTH | DESIGN | LLOY HACK ASSOCIATES

Keep built-in features in proportion to your room, as seen here in the low cubby-holes created for ceramics and books.

PHOTOGRAPHY | CAROL PEERCE | DESIGN | MARSHA SEWELL, ASID

Choose pieces of furniture that are the right size for tiny areas. Here, a table is nestled in front of a fireplace, enabling traffic to get around it.

furniture

Be suspicious of step-by-step formulas for furniture arrangements. Look at your raw space and evaluate its architectural features, constraints, and peculiarities. You don't need an expert to tell you about the height of your ceilings, your limited wall space, or the location of the fireplace. You know better than anyone the traffic patterns of your home and how you would like to use each room. In small rooms, the most important characteristics of furniture are size and dimension. Interior designers use "in scale" and "out of scale" to describe pieces as acceptable or totally wrong for a particular space. Getting the size, look, and placement just right takes thought and keen observation.

If your room is limited in actual floor area but blessed with high ceilings, you might try larger sizes of furniture. Consider using relatively strong colors on walls if your room features large windows or French doors. But when your room has little natural light, take care to keep the feel of furnishings simple and delicate rather than substantial. There are times when a tiny room can charm with the sensation of overstuffed comfort, and other times when sleek simplicity is the solution. Balance furniture arrangements with symmetrically placed objects—two chairs opposite one sofa, for instance, or a heavy, bulky object countered by one that has strong, bold color. Art on a wall above a piece of furniture can provide needed balance or a shout of counterpoint that enlivens the atmosphere. Think about your purpose first and the position of furniture next. Try to be flexible; you may have to rid yourself of furniture that will not work, doesn't enhance your comfort or aesthetic experience, or blocks the successful use of an area.

A small-scale armchair is accompanied by a small side table. Make certain that the arms of your furniture are not eating up all the space. And keep in mind that everything does not have to match; in fact, it's better if it doesn't. Free yourself to use individual furniture pieces that are the right style for the look.

PHOTOGRAPHY
CAROL PEERCE
DESIGN
MARSHA SEWELL, ASID

Even seemingly insignificant details like small display items or a well-placed sign can spice up a small room.

PHOTOGRAPHY
SAM GRAY PHOTOGRAPHY
DESIGN
BIERLY-DRAKE

An enclosed sun porch can become part of your interior space. This sitting area off the kitchen functions like a small family room. Once again, the ottoman appears as a coffee table.

PHOTOGRAPHY
JEFF McNAMARA
DESIGN
AUSTIN PATTERSON DISSTON

(right) A bay window is a wonderful place to display art without interfering with the flow of traffic in a room.

PHOTOGRAPHY
CAROL PEERCE
DESIGN
MARSHA SEWELL, ASID

Sometimes one well-chosen piece is all you need to complete a small space. In this case, it's a bench that has a lot of character. You can also try a narrow table or shallow cabinet.

PHOTOGRAPHY
COLL PHOTOGRAPHY
DESIGN
DOREE FRIEDMAN

This room combines honest symmetry with bold lines. The furniture is simple and architectural in feel but not out of scale with the space. Choose a few strong furniture pieces to communicate your look clearly.

PHOTOGRAPHY
POLIFORM

Antiques suit small, traditional rooms. Pieces like the bed seen here were originally designed with little floor space and high ceilings in mind. The scale in this bedroom is perfect.

PHOTOGRAPHY
ERIC A. ROTH
DESIGN
PETER WHEELER

Tiny does not equal boring. Here, a small bench is placed at one end of the dining table surrounded by armless chairs. Experiment with chair frames and fabrics that don't match for a tasty solution to furnishing a small dining room.

PHOTOGRAPHY | **ERIC A. ROTH** | DESIGN | **PAT STAVARIDIS**

Switch living and dining furniture, and dine in front of your fireplace. Instead of a sofa and chairs, four comfortable armchairs ring an upholstered ottoman coffee table. Try replacing bulky sofas with chairs; guests prefer their own personal space anyway.

Pull furniture away from the perimeter of your room and angle it to make it look more interesting. If the size of the pieces is correct, it will not matter that the room is small.

PHOTOGRAPHY
ERIC A. ROTH
DESIGN
DOMAIN HOME FURNISHINGS

Revisit the idea of symmetrical and traditional room arrangements, but break the old rules. Use furniture to break up a small room into separate, functional areas.

PHOTOGRAPHY
ERIC A. ROTH
DESIGN
MANUEL de SANTAREN, INC.

Antique shops are great places
to look for small-scale furniture
like the pieces pictured here.

PHOTOGRAPHY
ERIC A. ROTH
DESIGN
ROBERT MIKLOS

Place a simple oversize chair with floor cushions in front of a fireplace for a cozy effect. Try different types of floor pillows or low benches, which are unobtrusive, for a variety of casual seating arrangements.

PHOTOGRAPHY
JEFF McNAMARA
DESIGN
AUSTIN PATTERSON DISSTON

Minimalism has a place in small quarters like this guest room. Treat the entire wall behind the beds as one unit, creating a fluid, wall-to-wall and floor-to-ceiling "headboard." The room is unified and stretched visually as a result.

PHOTOGRAPHY
THE ROGER WILLIAMS HOTEL
DESIGN
UNIQUE HOTELS AND RESORTS

Hunt for an interesting bench, such as the one used here, to act as a very narrow coffee table. Benches are the perfect scale for a tight space and are easy to find.

PHOTOGRAPHY
ERIC A. ROTH
DESIGN
PETER WHEELER

Consider using an ottoman that can double as a coffee table. You'll want to select a durable fabric; this one's covered in raffia. Velvet and silk are gorgeous but not practical in this instance. Try leather, synthetic woven materials, and textures that disguise soiling.

PHOTOGRAPHY
SAM GRAY PHOTOGRAPHY
DESIGN
BIERLY-DRAKE

Attic rooms produce unusual challenges and space. This upstairs bedroom in a 450-square-foot (42-square-meter) cottage has just the right size furniture. Notice the delicacy in the vintage iron bed frame and petite side tables.

PHOTOGRAPHY
SAM GRAY PHOTOGRAPHY
DESIGN
BIERLY-DRAKE

If you light the space under a stairway properly, it can become a great spot for a home desk. This little work area is suited to writing correspondence and paying bills. An area like this could also be designed with custom built-ins for a computer workstation.

PHOTOGRAPHY
ERIC A. ROTH
DESIGN
PETER WHEELER

A simple side table can be
dressed with a table skirt and
double as a sideboard for a
dining area.

PHOTOGRAPHY
ERIC A. ROTH
DESIGN
PAT STAVARIDIS

kitchens AND BATHS

Kitchens and bathrooms represent a relatively large investment because of their appliances, plumbing, and water-resistant surfaces, but they can be more than simply utilitarian. Any realtor will tell you that the kitchen and master bath can hook buyers.

Just as the hearth of days past symbolized home, love, and family, the kitchen is the heart of the contemporary house. Food preparation and the enjoyment of sharing meals together are basic pleasures, ones that might be spoiled if quarters are tight and equipment lacking. The smaller the space, the more carefully you'll have to analyze and plan it.

Fortunately, small appliances are available. There are single refrigerated drawers, single-drawer dishwashers, and miniature microwaves and stoves. Also, home-improvement stores offer many devices to utilize every square inch of any living space.

Current trends in bathroom design include sleek, sculpture-like sinks that perch on pedestals or hang off the wall. Colored glass bowls and antique chests are being used in place of uncomplicated white fixtures and pullmans. You can adorn walls with waterproof faux painting or trompe l'oeil decorations, and use marble, limestone, slate, or granite in addition to ceramic tile. Lighting options have improved, as has the range of medicine cabinets available.

PHOTOGRAPHY | **BRADY ARCHITECTURAL PHOTOGRAPHY** | DESIGN | **DESIGN INSTITUTE OF SAN DIEGO STUDENTS**

Here, a wall-mounted faucet helps to conserve space. Achieve a handcrafted look to add to the coziness of the room by choosing the right materials. In this case, slate, natural teak wood, and limestone combine to create an earthy texture.

(left/right) The sleek, clean lines of this kitchen go a long way toward making it feel spacious. Storage under the island and above the appliances keeps items out of the way but within reach.

PHOTOGRAPHY
JEFF McNAMARA
DESIGN
AUSTIN PATTERSON DISSTON

A U-shaped kitchen can accommodate a breakfast bar instead of a nook. Consider angling or raising ceilings whenever possible, as seen here, to add the illusion of space.

PHOTOGRAPHY
STEVE VIERRA PHOTOGRAPHY
DESIGN
GAYLE REYNOLDS

The problem of having little floor space can be countered with ceilings that soar. Here, the high ceilings make the black wall behind the range's upper cabinets work.

PHOTOGRAPHY
BRADY ARCHITECTURAL PHOTOGRAPHY
DESIGN
JIM WALTERS, ASID

Powder baths can be squeezed into odd spaces; here's one under a staircase. Make the most from odd architectural shapes with the addition of a small art niche like this.

PHOTOGRAPHY
ED GOHLICH
DESIGN
MARYCLARE BRANDT, ASID

Free up floor space with a pedestal sink with towel bars attached. A low-profile toilet fixture also helps streamline the room.

PHOTOGRAPHY
COLL PHOTOGRAPHY
DESIGN
DOREE FRIEDMAN

Eliminate the need for bulky window treatments by incorporating safety glass or even trying obscure types of glass. Research options at your local glass shop.

PHOTOGRAPHY
ED GOHLICH
DESIGN
MARYCLARE BRANDT, ASID

Here, an odd architectural space becomes a graceful tub area. Use artwork freely in a bathroom, as you would in any other room of the house.

PHOTOGRAPHY
ERIC A. ROTH

PHOTOGRAPHY | **DAVID HENDERSON**

There's no need to sacrifice style when working with a small kitchen. This built-in, for example, has all the charm of an antique.

PHOTOGRAPHY | **COLL PHOTOGRAPHY** | DESIGN | **DOREE FRIEDMAN**

Try a tile design detail like the one seen here for subtle accent in a small kitchen. The detail mimics the prairie-style French doors.

Kitchen nooks may be the only dining space in a small home. Lend them some formality by dressing the windows, and arrange art on the walls.

PHOTOGRAPHY
ERIC A. ROTH

Today's gadgets surpass the storage concepts of the 1920s. Include a pullout pantry if you lack the space for a more typical opening-door type.

PHOTOGRAPHY
BRADY ARCHITECTURAL PHOTOGRAPHY
DESIGN
LAURA BIRNS, ASID

You can pop in a mini–built-in china closet or buffet in a small kitchen and dress up the area, as seen in this little corner.

PHOTOGRAPHY
STEVE VIERRA PHOTOGRAPHY
DESIGN
TAMMY COUTURE

The starkness of this bathroom delivers a kind of tranquility appreciated when there's not much extra space. Consider a very simple approach as a foundation for a calm, orderly bathroom.

PHOTOGRAPHY
JEFF McNAMARA
DESIGN
AUSTIN PATTERSON DISSTON

Try a shine-free sleek look to keep things simple in a small space. Use honed marble, lime-stone, or granite to achieve a matte surface. (Be sure to seal these porous materials regularly.)

PHOTOGRAPHY
JEFF McNAMARA
DESIGN
AUSTIN PATTERSON DISSTON

Although this room isn't very large, it packs a lot of punch, with its unique centerpiece and clean-lined furniture.

Try using several tiles together in one room to add texture and interest without cutting into precious space. Consider their overall tone and compatibility as you make your selections.

PHOTOGRAPHY
ED GOHLICH
DESIGN
MARYCLARE BRANDT, ASID

Rich color wraps this room; the same tone is successfully used in the wall covering, tile floor, and tub walls. Select color without fear, and contrast it with crisp white fixtures and cabinetry to make a small space sparkle.

PHOTOGRAPHY
ED GOHLICH
DESIGN
MARYCLARE BRANDT, ASID

Once you get a brilliant idea, it's sometimes a chore to actually locate a product that fits your needs. Custom design is not always feasible; either your budget cannot support such luxury, or you need a faster solution. Luckily, plenty of products have been developed with flexibility and dual function in mind.

Habitat magazines are chock-full of ads for these products, and many companies list 800 numbers and e-mail addresses, making it easy and inexpensive to contact them. The Internet has opened worldwide access to hundreds of brilliant designs. From Denmark, for example, come free-standing wood-burning stoves that occupy little floor space, with units that average about 21 inches deep, 25 inches wide, and 34 inches to 47 inches high (53 by 64 by 86 to 119 cm).

Other gadgets are perfect for expanding the efficiency of limited space.Try a built-in ironing center in a bedroom closet or the kitchen, wall-mounted hair dryers like the ones in hotel rooms, or wall systems for storing kitchen utensils. Install wall-mounted lid racks and undershelf wire baskets. Seek out pull-out trash bins, recycling baskets, and pantry-door racks. And tour antique shops; they're good sources of small-scale pieces.

design ideas

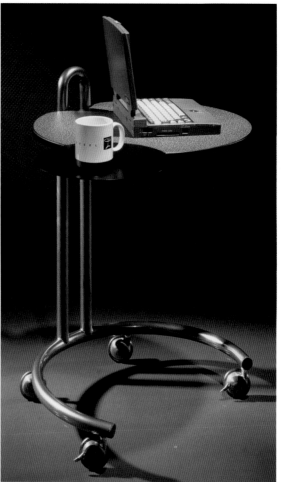

Consider an open bookcase or étagère as a room divider. It's both practical and aesthetically pleasing. You can even load the shelves with plants to create a wall of green.

PHOTOGRAPHY
M.T. MAXWELL FURNITURE CO.

This whimsical little mobile table, aptly named Rover, is ideal for homes that can't accommodate traditional office furniture.

PHOTOGRAPHY
VERSTEEL

The Tristano bed is available in a
version with a chassis; in this
case, the bedstead can be lifted
up, and the chassis becomes a
useful under-bed storage area.

PHOTOGRAPHY
POLIFORM
DESIGN
POLIFORM DESIGN CENTER

Scout for multipurpose furniture,
like this drawer seat.

PHOTOGRAPHY
JOHN KELLY
DESIGN
JOHN KELLY

This versatile 58 by 36 inch (147 by 91 cm) dining table and four chairs fold away into a compact sideboard when not in use.

PHOTOGRAPHY
HAMMACHER SCHLEMMER
DESIGN
HAMMACHER SCHLEMMER

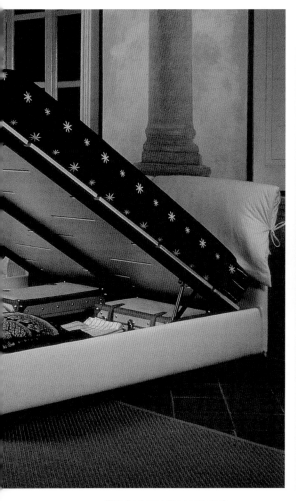

This bed uses the same technology as a convertible Mercedes-Benz to reveal its secret compartment.

PHOTOGRAPHY
DORMIRE
DESIGN
VICO MAGESTRETTI

This tiny table, called Rover Senior, is sleek and unobtrusive yet functional.

PHOTOGRAPHY
VERSTEEL
DESIGN
VERSTEEL

Imagine a dishwasher in a single
drawer, small enough to fit into
the most cramped kitchen area.
You can use one for dirty dishes
and one for clean.

PHOTOGRAPHY
FISHER & PAYKEL
DESIGN
FISHER & PAYKEL

Stacking chairs from 'vik-ter II
can solve the problem of what to
do when extra guests invade your
small home. Roll guest seating
into a closet for compact storage.

PHOTOGRAPHY
DAKOTA JACKSON, INC.
DESIGN
DAKOTA JACKSON, INC.

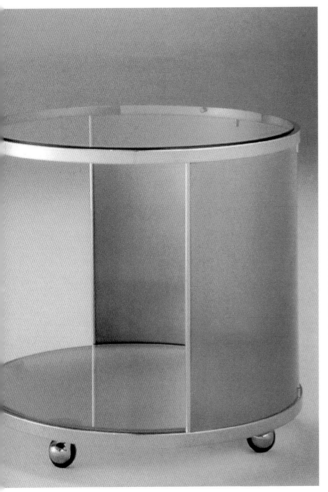

Look for clean and simple designs, which tend to eliminate visual clutter.

PHOTOGRAPHY
BRUETON STUDIO
DESIGN
CHARLES GIBILTERRA

Select small, mobile upholstered pieces like these, which can go anywhere.

PHOTOGRAPHY
BONAVENTURE USA
DESIGN
STANLEY JAY FRIEDMAN

Organize your closets to take
advantage of vertical space.

PHOTOGRAPHY
POLIFORM
DESIGN
POLIFORM DESIGN CENTER

Capture every inch of closet
space. The back of the door can
hold racks and hooks, while wire
drawer units can accommodate
folded clothing under short
hanging garments.

PHOTOGRAPHY
THE CONTAINER STORE

Choose a coffee table that
rolls, like this one, so you
can easily reorganize a small
space as needed.

PHOTOGRAPHY
BRUETON STUDIO
DESIGN
STANLEY JAY FRIEDMAN

Try solving pint-size problems
with adjustable systems like this
that are flexible enough to
change as your child grows from
toddler to teenager.

PHOTOGRAPHY
THE CONTAINER STORE

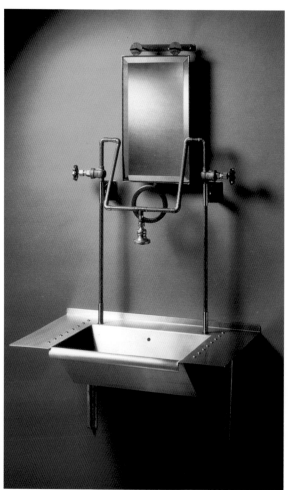

Look for contemporary pieces in the appropriate proportion for your small rooms—not too deep or too wide. This tallboy is a good example.

PHOTOGRAPHY
M.T. MAXWELL FURNITURE CO.

A lack of floor space shouldn't keep you from high style. Use a wall-mounted sink-and-mirror combo like this one, which is of Italian design.

PHOTOGRAPHY
HASTINGS
DESIGN
IL BAGNO

This countertop unit bakes, broils, steams, roasts, and sautés using high-energy halogen lights. The size of a microwave, it works in half the time of a regular oven and takes up a fraction of the space.

PHOTOGRAPHY
FLASHBAKE

This open square bookcase offers a geometric home for books and treasures and can double as an ample room divider.

PHOTOGRAPHY
KOHLER CO./BAKER
DESIGN
MICHAEL VANDERBYL

Look for maximum efficiency in bath accessory products, like this "laser." The unit provides tiny glass shelves, a shaving mirror, a light, and handy towel racks.

PHOTOGRAPHY
IL BAGNO
DESIGN
HERBERT LUDWIKOWSKI (LASER)
BERGER + STAHL (BASIN)

Portable screens, like this dressing screen, can be useful and are convenient. Use them to block an open kitchen from the dining-room area or sleeping quarters from the living room.

PHOTOGRAPHY
JOHN KELLY
DESIGN
JOHN KELLY

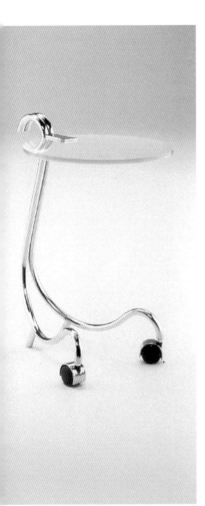

Find functional items that also have panache and style, like this space-saving table.

PHOTOGRAPHY
BRUETON STUDIO
DESIGN
STANLEY JAY FRIEDMAN

This Gepettto table looks like it's about to start walking. Stylized tables such as this one have a personality of their own but don't require a lot of space.

PHOTOGRAPHY
BRUETON STUDIO
DESIGN
STANLEY JAY FRIEDMAN

Ali A. Alam
1431-B Colorado Avenue
Santa Monica, CA 90404

Austin Patterson Disston
Architects, LLC
376 Pequot Avenue
Southport, CT 06490

B & B Italia, USA, Inc.
150 East 58th Street
New York, NY 10155

Bast/Wright Interiors
307 Eighth Avenue
San Diego, CA 92101

Bierly-Drake & Associates
17 Arlington Street
Boston, MA 02116

Laura Birns, ASID
P.O. Box 812
Del Mar, CA 92014

Jim Brady
BRADY Architectural Photography
1010 University Avenue #823
San Diego, CA 92103

MaryClare Brandt, ASID
MC Brandt Interior Design
P.O. Box 8276
La Jolla, CA 92083-8276

Carol G. Brown, ASID
7541 Eads Avenue
La Jolla, CA 92037

Brueton Studio
Brueton Industries, Inc.
145-68 228th Street
Springfield Gardens, NY 11413-3934

Kim Brun Studios
9605 S.W. Ventura Court
Tigard, OR 97223

Coll Photography
1715 9th Street
Berkeley, CA 94710

The Container Store
2000 Valwood Parkway
Dallas, TX 75234-8800

Dormire
Francesca Bianchi
1345 4th Street
Santa Monica, CA 90401

Beverly Feldman, ASID
13841 Etude Road
San Diego, CA 92128

Fisher & Paykel Appliances, Inc.
22982 Alcalde Drive, Suite 201
Laguna Hills, CA 92653

FlashBake
47817 Fremont Boulevard
Fremont, CA 94538

KraftMaid Cabinetry, Inc.
P.O. Box 1055
15535 South State Avenue
Middlefield, OH 44062

Doree Friedman
Fineline Construction
1615 Cortland Street
San Francisco, CA 94110

Stanley Jay Friedman
c/o Bruteon Industries
145-68 228th Street
Springfield Gardens, NY 11413-3934

Charles Gibilterra
c/o Bruteon Industries
145-68 228th Street
Springfield Gardens, NY 11413-3934

Ed Gohlich
P.O. Box 180919
Coronado, CA 92178

Sam Gray Photography
374 Congress Street
Boston, MA 02210

Grey Crawford Photography
2924 Park Center Drive
Los Angeles, CA 90068

Hammacher Schlemmer
303 West Erie Street
Chicago, IL 60610

Hastings Tile/Il Bagno Collection/Kitchen Studio
Kitchen Studio
30 Commercial Street
Freeport, NY 11520

Diane Hughes Interiors
Seacoast Village
29 Lafayette Road
North Hampton, NH 03862

Hydra Designs
720 Monroe Street, C-102
Hoboken, NJ 07030

The Iron Shop
P.O. Box 547
400 Reed Road
Broomall, PA 19008

Charlotte S. Jensen, ASID
11464 Escoba Place
San Diego, CA 92127-1015

Johnson Hardware
2100 Sterling Avenue
Elkhart, IN 44516

John Kelly Furniture
144 Chambers Street
New York, NY 10007

KraftMaid Cabinetry, Inc.
P.O. Box 1055
15535 South State Avenue
Middlefield, OH 44062

Susan Lefkowitz
Ann Lenox
Herbert Ludwikowski
Vico Magestretti
Brenda Lanza, ASID
13279 Vinter Way
Poway, CA 92064-1216

Jeffrey Alan Marks
7746 Herschel Avenue
La Jolla, CA 92037
and
1007 Montana Avenue
Santa Monica, CA 90403

Marylin Mattson
The J.H. Wolfe Company, Inc.
833-A South Main Street, #396
Fallbrook, CA 92028

Owen McGoldrick Photography
2103 29th Street
San Diego, CA 92104

Jeff McNamara
68 Vista
Easton, CT 06612

Linda Medina, ASID
3255 Talbot Street
San Diego, CA 92106

M.T. Maxwell Furniture Co.
715 Liberty St.
Bedford, VA 24523

Carol Peerce
7043 Enders Avenue
San Diego, CA 92122

Poliform USA, Inc.
150 East 58th Street, Floor 9
New York, NY 10155

Anjum Razvi, ASID
14829 Pensaquitos Court
San Diego, CA 92129

Eric A. Roth
Henderson Studio
337 Summer Street
Boston, MA 02210

Sauder Woodworking Co.
502 Middle Street
Archbold, OH 43502

Marsha Sewell, ASID
629 5th Avenue
San Diego, CA 92101

Dawn P. Sullivan, Allied Member ASID
P.O. Box 301113
Escondido, CA 92030-1113

Unique Hotels and Resorts
840 Apollo Street, Suite 314
El Segundo, CA 90245

Versteel
P.O. Box 850
Jasper, IN 47547

Steve Vierra
P.O. Box 1827
Sandwich, MA 02563

Jim Walters, ASID
5000 Bristol Road
San Diego, CA 92116

Kathleen M. Zbacnik, ASID
7556 Fay Avenue
La Jolla, CA 92037

This book would not have been possible without Charlie, my best friend and husband, who believed that I could be a writer before I knew it was true. He is in every breath I take and every word I write.

Acknowledgments

A special thanks to Jack Regan, my good friend from Boston, for his gracious professional assistance, and to Sister Bernadette, my first- and seventh-grade teacher, who taught me how to write and encouraged me. Gratitude is also extended to all of the photographers who have accommodated their designer-clients, and a special thank you to each architect and interior designer whose work is displayed in the book. These professionals put more into their work than anyone can know, and to freeze the results in a picture is to tell only half the story.

About the author

Christine Brun Abdelnour is a professional member of the American Society of Interior Designers and a practicing certified interior designer in the state of California. As a syndicated columnist for the Copley News Service, she writes a weekly column entitled "Small Spaces" that appears in over twenty newspapers in the U.S. and abroad. For nearly twenty years she has managed her own interior design firm, Christine Brun & Associates, located in La Jolla, CA.